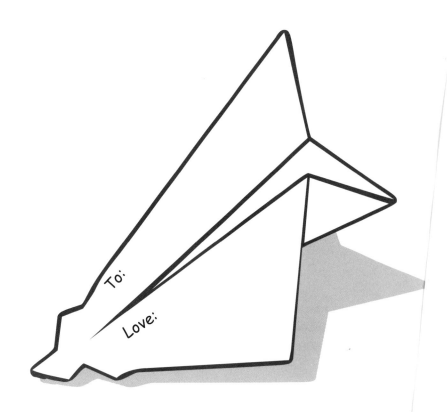

To:

Love:

Brothers
Are Special

COMPILED BY
LUCY MEAD

GRAMERCY BOOKS
NEW YORK

This 2004 edition is published by Gramercy Books, an imprint of Random House Value
Publishing, a division of Random House, Inc., New York.

Gramercy is a registered trademark and the colophon is a trademark of Random House, Inc.

Random House
New York • Toronto • London • Sydney • Auckland
www.randomhouse.com

Interior design: Karen Ocker Design, New York

Printed and bound in Singapore

Library of Congress Cataloging-in-Publication Data

Brothers are special : a tribute to those who love, nurture, and inspire / compiled
   by Lucy Mead.
       p. cm.
    ISBN 0-517-22428-3
     1. Brothers—Quotations, maxims, etc. 2. Brothers—Poetry. I. Mead, Lucy.

 PN6084.B7B767 2004
 306.875—dc22

                                                                    2004042504

10 9 8 7 6 5 4 3 2

Brothers
Are Special

Groucho: You love your brother, don't you?
Chico: No, but I'm used to him.

from the movie *Go West*

The folks sent me a clipping of you taking the oath. The sight of
you up there was really moving, particularly as a close examination
showed that you had my checked London coat on. I'd like to
know what the hell I'm doing out here while you go stroking
around in my drape coat, but I supposed that's what we are out
here for—so that our sisters and younger brothers will be safe and
secure—frankly, I don't see it quite that way. At least, if you're
going to be safe and secure, that's fine with me, but not in my
coat, brother, not in my coat.

JACK KENNEDY to Bobby Kennedy, from the Solomon Islands, 1944

Sibling rivalry in our family began the first day I brought
our second son home from the hospital. His brother
looked at him and said, "Maybe later we could get a dog."

ERMA BOMBECK, *Family—The Ties That Bind...and Gag*

It was a happy moment for me when, at almost six, I discovered that my folks had gotten me a baby brother. When Melvin got big enough to play with me, we bonded for a lifetime.

BILLY GRAHAM, *Just As I Am*

I went to my father's garden,
And found an Irish farthing.
I gave it to my mother
To buy a baby brother.
My brother was so nasty,
I baked him in a pasty,
The pasty wasn't tasty
So I threw it over the garden wall,
I threw it over the garden wall.

English rhyme in Nancy Friday's,
Our Looks, Our Lives

...belligerent, I think is a good word.

PAUL NEWMAN describing his
childhood relationship with his brother

The most vivid emotion of my childhood, the one I can evoke even now, is my hatred of my brother Bob. ...A virtual rainbow of negative emotions—contempt, loathing, disdain—that is how I remember my life with my brother from the time he improbably arrived, cradled in my mother's arms when I was little more than a year old. It's like remembering a wonderful meal or a remarkable painting, remembering how much I hated Bob, then called by the diminutive "Robbie."

ANNA QUINDLEN, *Siblings*

The younger brother hath the more wit.
ENGLISH PROVERB

Of course, I registered for the draft right away. They asked me in such a way I couldn't refuse. They were gonna draft my brother, but there was a little confusion. His body was one-A, but his brain was four-F.

BOB HOPE

Then there is your brother—6 feet four inches tall, lovable and intelligent. You fought with him when you were little, threw tin soldiers at his head, gouged his neck with a careless flick of your ice skate…and then last summer, as you worked on the farm, you grew to love him, confide in him, and know him as a person.

SYLVIA PLATH, *Unabridged Journals*

It's tough to play your sibling. My brother and I are real close and I was thinking last night, if we were the same gender and in the semifinals having to play each other, my God, I would hate it.

BILLIE JEAN KING

He's a terrific guy and the world's quietest person. The night he broke (Lou) Gehrig's record, he went out and painted the town beige.

BILLY RIPKEN, on his brother, Cal

What can I do about Ron? He's ruining us. I know we should drop him. But how can I? He's my brother and he's mad.

REGGIE KRAY of the Kray Twins

We are all brothers under our pelts.

OGDEN NASH

I ate from the same table as Albert and came from the same womb but I know he killed many men and he deserved to die.

ANTHONY "TOUGH TONY" ANASTASIA in *New York Magazine*

Dear Ann Landers: Every year at Christmas, my brother sends me frozen steaks from a catalog company. The steaks cost him at least $60. I can buy those same steaks at my local grocery store for $15.

How can I tell him that I do not appreciate his expensive, totally impersonal gift? I know he sends the same thing to his clients and business associates. Is he so lazy that he cannot shop for his only sister? Maybe I should keep my mouth shut, but every time I think about it, it burns me up. Any suggestions?

BIG SISTER

Dear Big Sister: A gift is whatever someone chooses to send. These days, many people prefer to "shop" via catalog or over the Internet. Kwitcherbeefin' about the beef, and don't sweat the small stuff, Sis. At least he is thinking about you.

ANN

Six years old when [my brother] Ethan was born, I recall no feelings of jealousy. Though losing my status as an only child, all I remember is my excitement, that our estate would now contain another small person, and perhaps I would not feel so lonesome. My mother recalls it different. When Ethan was born, she says my first words upon seeing him in the hospital were, "Look, Mommy, I hurt my finger."

AISSA WAYNE, daughter of John Wayne

It never made a bit of difference to me that Hubert became an assistant United States attorney, a judge, and all that. He was still my little brother.

BESSIE DELANEY, *Having Our Say*

When she [Whoopi Goldberg] finally found her voice and gave her acceptance speech, she admitted that she had wanted an Oscar ever since she was a child. "My brother's sitting out there," she told the audience, saying, 'Thank God, we don't have to listen to her anymore.'"

ROSE BLUE and CORINNE J. NADEN, *Whoopi Goldberg*

I look back and I can remember a time when I used to sneak into my brother's room, rummage through his closet, and dig up his well hidden comics. They were kept in a briefcase for some odd reason…and they were one of those small treasures that we all had during our childhood. *The Adventures of Superman, Spiderman, Batman, Fantastic Four, The Incredible Hulk,* and of course, *the X-Men.*

KEN MIYAMOTO, *Entertainment Insiders*

People forget, the original Osmond Brothers had a large number of hits before the success of *Donny and Marie.* They went from having 47 gold and platinum records to appearing on the *Donny and Marie Show* dressed in lobster suits! That took a tremendous toll on my brothers.

JIMMY OSMOND

My brother Randy—the only other little Moffitt—was born in 1948, when I was five, and dad started to work with him too as soon as he was old enough. When I started to play tennis, Randy was about six and our household was a mess. Randy was practicing his pitching…and during the day I'd walk around with my tennis racket and try to practice my serve without knocking over too many lamps.

BILLIE JEAN KING

[My brother] Steve and I were not yet baseball crazy the October I got my first glove, but that next spring, Tom Hardey, an older cousin Steve and I looked up to, began playing organized ball, so we figured that baseball was probably a good thing for us to do too.

DAVE WINFIELD

A brother is a friend given by nature.

GABRIEL MARIE LEGOUVE, *Maxims*

Of all the friendships between brothers that I've known, and there have been many, none came close to that of the six Eisenhower boys. Partly that was because of their parents, partly because of their semi-rural setting, partly because there were so many of them and they had no sisters….They grew up without money or any possessions, only each other. And although they had some friends in the little town of Abilene, Kansas, where they lived, mainly they had to rely on each other.

STEPHEN E. AMBROSE, *Comrades*

The man who begins by asking you how many brothers and sisters you have is never a sympathetic character, and if you meet him in a year's time he will probably ask you how many brothers and sisters you have, his mouth again sagging open, his eyes still bulging from his head.

HERMAN MELVILLE

My brother, Benjamin, was born on October 6, 1953, so we are only a year and eleven days apart. My father and his younger brother, Richard, had a similar separation in age, and similar problems: in both cases the older one usually got the first crack at everything and was often preferred.

CHRISTOPHER REEVE, *Still Me*

Brothers resemble hands and feet.

CHINESE PROVERB

By now, my brother Paul had been born, to be followed in quick succession by Edward, Samuel, and the baby, Daniel. Dad no longer insisted on giving his kids romantic Arabic as well as Christian names. After me, Muzyad the Extraordinary, the children—from Emily on down—had names that were the same in Arabic as in English. A bigger problem was to find enough room for everyone—even with tripling up in the beds.

DANNY THOMAS

He [my brother] says what most people are thinking.

ELLEN STERN in *Howard Stern*

My oldest brother, Clarence…was a wonderful center fielder and, something I never was, a hitter. I used to think of him when I'd see that little Albie Pearson who played for the California Angels in the early Sixties. Clarence was just about Pearson's size, he could field every bit as good and had a lot more power. Enormous power for a little man. But Clarence was also a brilliant student, and he had the sense of responsibility that you find in oldest sons. He…went to work at the bottom rung of one of the biggest manufacturing companies in Springfield and ended up as executive vice-president.

LEO DUROCHER

My older brothers were pretty good ball players too. And when they had a chance to go play the game of baseball professionally, Dad wouldn't let them....As I was growing up, my skills as a baseball player grew tremendously....My older brothers recognized my talents and they did all that they could to convince my dad to let me play. They said, "We're all working here in the brickyard. Why don't you give him a chance to play?"

YOGI BERRA

I didn't start playing baseball until I was 14. My brother Luis was the one who played, and he introduced me to the game. He saw my talent and got me involved in Little League.

SAMMY SOSA

Verily, the name of brother is a glorious name,
and full of loving kindness.

MONTAIGNE, *Essays*

The upright had scarcely been put in place when George twirled
the stool down to size, sat, lifted the keyboard cover, and played
an accomplished version of a then popular song. I remember
being particularly impressed by his swinging left hand and by
harmonic and rhythmic effects I thought as proficient as those
of most of the pianists I'd heard in vaudeville.

IRA GERSHWIN

In form and feature, face and limb,
I grew so like my brother
That folks got taking me for him
And each for one another

H.S. LEIGH "The Twins"

I tried to understand what [my brother] Henry had told me. But I worried about that, too. Other people might not try as hard as I did to understand him. I was always on his side, no matter what…It scared me to think that my brother had failed at loving someone. I had no idea myself how to do it.

MELISSA BANK, *The Girls' Guide to Hunting and Fishing*

Lucy: What's the matter with you, big brother? You look like you just swallowed a chocolate cake…

Charlie Brown: They're going to give me a testimonial dinner! All the kids that I play baseball with are going to give me a testimonial dinner!

Lucy: Check the calendar…it must be April Fool's Day!

CHARLES SCHULTZ

When you're related to a celebrity—five of them, in this case—it's hard to truly comprehend the magnitude of their fame. To me, Jackie, Tito, Jermaine, Marlon, and Michael were just normal guys….I went to see them headline the Los Angeles Forum in June 1970. Hearing eighteen thousand teenagers and preteens (some with their parents) screaming hysterically for the Jackson 5, I looked around awestruck and wondered, This is for MY BROTHERS?

LA TOYA JACKSON, *Growing Up in the Jackson Family*

Brothers are one of those childhood treasures that we spend capriciously, only to learn their true value later.

RON, AGE 44

When we were very young our parents used to dress us alike.
Later I often joked that the only way you could tell us apart was
that I had the blue mittens and [my brother] Ben had the red
ones…We were often referred to as Tophy and Beejy. I remember
wanting to separate myself quite early on, and I think Ben did too.

CHRISTOPHER REEVE, *Still Me*

I was freckled—wore my hair like a boy's. In fact, with one
brother Tom older and two younger, Dick and Bob, being a
girl was a torment. I'd always wanted to be a boy. Jimmy was
my name, if you want to know.

KATHARINE HEPBURN

My older brother was the apple of my mother's eye. He always got the best part of the roast and the best part of the chicken, which means a lot to children. My younger brother, who was born many years later, was then spoiled all over. My mother favored the boys. You could hear the mothers talking when they were expecting. They always thought it was going to be a boy and hoped it was a boy.

DOROTHY SOMMER, 88, *Generations*

I am the oldest child, and even though I have a sister and two brothers, I have always considered myself the only child.

Surprised? Don't be. There isn't an eldest child alive who doesn't secretly think the same thing....

ALEX WITCHEL, *Girls Only*

Aw, Dad, all I ever do around here is retrieve Burt.

WILLIE LANCASTER about his brother Burt

My first [memory] is of being spanked for taking a toy train away from Bobby. I must have been about five. I can see him — his bright white hair, his merry blue eyes, his amazingly beautiful baby eyebrows—teetering around the room in a blue romper. Someone picked me up and paddled me. Mother? Daddy? Dott? My aunt Mary Eula, for whom I had been named Mary?

I quickly got over it because I adored him and must have known, down in my heart, that he would become the companion of my youth. He was to be my real life shining star, but this is the very first I even recall of his existence.

LIZ SMITH

My dear Bro.,

Every man must learn his trade—not pick it up. God requires
that he learn it by slow and painful processes. The apprentice
hand in blacksmithing, in medicine, in literature, in everything,
is a thing that can't be hidden. It always shows....This work of
yours is exceedingly crude but I am free to say it is less crude
than I expected it to be. And considerably better work than
I believed you could do.

> Yr Bro.
> Sam (Mark Twain)

Believe not your own brother—believe,
instead, you own blind eye.
RUSSIAN PROVERB

The brotherhood of men does not imply their equality. Families have their fools and their men of genius, their black sheep and their saints, their worldly successes and their worldly failures. A man should treat his brothers lovingly and with justice, according to the desserts of each. But the desserts of every brother are not the same.

ALDOUS HUXLEY

I have shot mine arrow o'er the house,
And hurt my brother.

SHAKESPEARE, *Hamlet. Act v. Sc. 2.*

I want to be the white man's brother, not his brother-in-law.

MARTIN LUTHER KING, JR.

A LOT like The Brady Bunch on crack.

STEPHEN BALDWIN describing his childhood
relationship with his brothers

When brothers have once broken the bonds of Nature, they can
come together again only with difficulty, and even if they do,
their reconciliation bears with it a filthy hidden sore of suspicion.

PLUTARCH, *Morals*

I have never heard any man mention his brother.
The subject seems distasteful to most men.

OSCAR WILDE

Ask [my brother] Harpo how much he's made and that's how much I've lost.

CHICO MARX

Early Thursday morning I walked in to rehearse the orchestra. Since I was the only one of the boys who didn't know an eighth note from a banknote, I never quite understood why I was delegated for this job. In later years I realized it was because I was the only Marx Brother who could be routed out of bed before noon.

GROUCHO MARX

Brothers quarrel like thieves inside a house, but outside their words leap out in each other's defense.

JAPANESE PROVERB

When I say to you that Dwight and I discussed every major decision he made, I must be sure you have this in mind: Most persons in leadership authority like to think out loud with someone he deems to be intelligent, well informed, conscious of all the nuances from fiscal policy to political possibility, can be trusted absolutely never to divulge a secret, and whom he admires: it is that kind of person who should be the President's principal confidant.

MILTON EISENHOWER

A lot of people criticize [my brother] Billy. But his standing in the public opinion polls is substantially above my own.

JIMMY CARTER

29

[My brother] Fred, though I loved him dearly, was not traditionally tough. He was sweet and trusting, and as a result, people constantly took advantage of him. Watching what happened to Fred, I learned to study people closely and always to keep my guard up, in both my personal and my professional life. Fred was truly one of my great teachers.

DONALD TRUMP

Like my brother Edward, [my brother] Charles had a severity of Character which did not permit him to be silly—no not for moments, but always self possessed & elegant whether morose or playful; no funning for him or for Edward.

RALPH WALDO EMERSON

Dearest father,
Darling mother,
How's my precious little brother?
Let me come home if you miss me.
I would even let Aunt Bertha hug and kiss me...

ALLAN SHERMAN, "Camp Grenada"

I grew up poor, living upstairs over my dad's dry cleaning and tailor shop. My father was incarcerated for bootlegging corn liquor he made in our basement when I was a senior in high school, leaving me to run the shop, go to school, and get about the business of being a good enough athlete so that I could get a scholarship to college and just be somebody. My brother James helped me quite a bit my senior year, giving me money when I really needed it and lending me some of his clothes.

REGGIE JACKSON

From the beginning, we called him [my brother] Chip, as in chip off the old block, and from the first day I saw him I loved him. At three and a half I wasn't really a baby myself anymore and could begin to grasp the idea of being his big sister, a role I loved. I'd stand by his playpen or crib and just watch him sleep for hours. People tell me I was very protective of Chip, even as a little girl. I still am today, even though he towers over me and protects me sometimes too.

VANNA WHITE

One thing I'll always remember about Adam was how dedicated he was to racing. We not only lost a fourth-generation driver, we lost a great friend and my brother. It's not the same without Adam here. Things will never be the same.

MONTGOMERY LEE PETTY

When we were kids we went to the same elementary school in Brooklyn N.Y., P.S. 159. [My brother] Eric was in the play the*Wizard of Oz*, which all his life was one of his favorite movies. We were in the school auditorium, and Eric was playing the part of the Scarecrow. Everything was going along fine, until the part where Dorothy tries to get him off the pole. He got stuck on the top. The curtains closed and all the teachers ran to the backstage area, and when the curtains opened again Eric was still on the pole. He remained there the whole show, it was hilarious, my sister and I never did let him forget it.

LORETTA CARAVELLO about her brother Eric Carr,
drummer for rock group Kiss

I asked my dad how much Adam made from the commercial…It just kept going through my head: My brother has fifty thousand dollars. That was my driving force. I remember for, like, five years thinking my brother was better than me because he had that.

LEONARDO DICAPRIO

...I tried to get back into the role of the older brother. Ron had gotten into a bad automobile accident...I suggested he travel with me for a month or so. Ours had always been a distant relationship, and it is still not what it should be, but at that moment we were both happy to be together. I think I wanted to share who I was and what I was doing with Ron, and I think he was open to finding out. Time was short, though, and all the traveling around kept us from really connecting on the level I had hoped we would....

JOHN DENVER, Take Me Home

[My brother] was constantly at the typewriter...got lots of rejection slips. If I remember correctly, there was a nail pounded in the wall up in the bedroom, and he'd spear all the rejection slips on it.

DAVID KING, brother of Stephen King

My dear Sister,

...if you have a brother nearly eighteen years of age who is not able to take care of himself a few miles from home, such a brother is not worth one's thoughts....I shall ask favors from no one, and endeavor to be as "independent as a wood-sawyer's clerk."

                    Truly your Brother
                    Sam (Mark Twain)

On weekend mornings, while most kids were up watching their favorite cartoons, my brothers and I were out rounding up grocery carts at a neighborhood supermarket. Later, my twin brother and I obtained our first real job working in a hardware store. Although we would come home exhausted, there was no feeling greater to us than being able to contribute to our family.

                    SAL, AGE 27

Concerned over my brother. A man who conveys a feeling of deep perplexity. Things have not turned out the way he meant them to. The way he speaks and looks, the mind that strikes almost always idly or in self-defense, the way he pares his fingernails and wipes his mouth on his sleeve…Sullen, contradictory, and laconic. I am troubled because he is my brother and because he has for years been the man of the family. Now all these transformations have left him incompetent.

JOHN CHEEVER, The Journals of John Cheever

Oh, call my brother back to me!
I cannot play alone:
The summer comes with flower and bee,—
Where is my brother gone?

FELICIA DOROTHEA (BROWNE) HEMANS,
"The Child's First Grief"

Photographer: Move over, you're in your brother's [Robert] shadow.
Ted Kennedy: That's the way it will be when we're in the Senate.

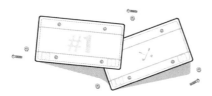

When reporters talk to Clint Howard, the question he must be asked a gazillion times is what it was like growing up with Opie—or Richie Cunningham, or famous director Ron Howard as his brother. "Ron's shadow is a pretty cool place to be. Hey, better to be Ron Howard's brother than to be Son of Sam's brother."

CLINT HOWARD

What Ted did does weigh heavily on us. I think we're hoping this will move us toward closure. It helps to feel that some small good came out of this tragedy.

DAVID KACYZNSKI on his brother, the Unabomber

...I could tell it was going to be a terrible, horrible, no good, very bad day.

At breakfast Anthony found a Corvette Sting Ray car kit in his breakfast cereal box and Nick found a Junior Undercover Agent code ring in his breakfast cereal box but in my breakfast cereal box all I found was breakfast cereal.

JUDITH VIORST, *Alexander and the Terrible, Horrible, No Good, Very Bad Day*

38

Of course I did hit Bob. Of course I could. He was my brother. That explains everything. If he was anyone else as different from me in interests and activities, I wouldn't even know him today... But he isn't anyone else.

ANNA QUINDLEN

While we're on the way to there
Why not share
And the load
Doesn't weigh me down at all
He ain't heavy, he's my brother.

He's my brother
He ain't heavy, he's my brother.

Written by B. SCOTT AND B. RUSSELL

From the time we were little children my brother Orville and myself lived together, played together, worked together and, in fact, thought together. We usually owned all our toys in common, talked over our thoughts and aspirations so that nearly everything that was done in our lives has been the result of conversations, suggestions and discussions between us.

WILBUR WRIGHT

I preferred to take care of [my brother] Stanley. For one thing, I liked the baby, and for another he was no particular trouble...He stayed in the carriage and I propped myself in a chair leaning back against the brick wall of the house, reading—and set to go into the store if I were called.

ISAAC ASIMOV

My brother Russell...understood me well. He understood that I had great moves in bed, where the two of us constantly fought for control of one small mattress. Night after night in the darkness of our bedroom, we were opponents in pajamas. Although I was six years older than Russell, I managed to be just as immature.

BILL COSBY

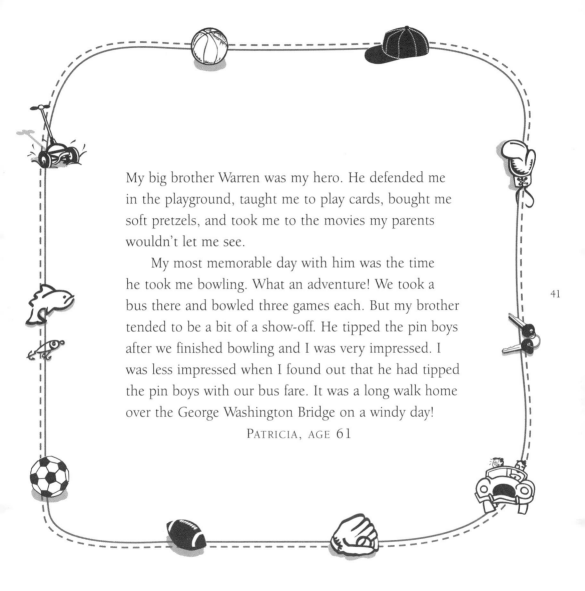

My big brother Warren was my hero. He defended me in the playground, taught me to play cards, bought me soft pretzels, and took me to the movies my parents wouldn't let me see.

My most memorable day with him was the time he took me bowling. What an adventure! We took a bus there and bowled three games each. But my brother tended to be a bit of a show-off. He tipped the pin boys after we finished bowling and I was very impressed. I was less impressed when I found out that he had tipped the pin boys with our bus fare. It was a long walk home over the George Washington Bridge on a windy day!

PATRICIA, AGE 61

Though a brother, he considered himself as my master and me as his apprentice, and accordingly expected the same services from me as he would from another; while I thought he degraded me too much in some he required of me, who from a brother expected more indulgences.

BENJAMIN FRANKLIN

I didn't know until recently that [my brother] Jamie missed a whole year at college. It just shows how clever and tight he was....I remember seeing him leave every morning for the campus, and I used to see him there myself that year, but I didn't know he wasn't going to classes....My guess now is that the way he spent his time was either to go to the library and read, or to head downtown and see a silent picture show.

ROBERT THURBER, brother of James Thurber

My brother Jonas, whom the world knows for his work with polio…came from his home in California to help care for me. During times of good health we saw and spoke with each other frequently. Now Jonas was there night and day…When I finally began to turn the corner and improve, my wife tells me that Jonas, who is a sensitive man, took my hand and wept quietly.

DR. LEE SALK, *Familyhood*

If anyone thinks it is a soft thing to be a commanding officer's brother he misses his guess.

TOM CUSTER about his brother, General Custer

The brothers became inseparable. There was a genuine fondness between them and no conflict about hogging the limelight. Fred by now had come to realize his brother's star quality and backed off comfortably into the supporting role. Gene was amused by his younger brother's attitude, his sheer delight in being onstage.

ALVIN YUDKOFF, *Gene Kelly*

If it wasn't you, it was your brother.
LA FONTAINE, "The Wolf and the Lamb"

Am I my brother's keeper?
GENESIS 4:9

"You are always harping upon it! What have I to do with it? Am I my brother Dmitri's keeper?"
DOSTOEVSKY, *The Brothers Karamazov*

But, when one has broken the bonds of nature, there is nothing that can reunite those whom knots so strong could not hold together. One hates with excess when one hates a brother.
RACINE, *The Enemy Brothers*

The brother whose aims are relative to himself
alone is neither brother nor relative.

SADI, *Gulistan*

Birds in their little nests agree
And 'tis a shameful sight,
When children of one family
Fall out, and chide, and fight.

ISAAC WATTS, "Love between
Brothers and Sisters"

Alan Frog: Kill your brother, you'll feel better.

Lost Boys

Seatmate on airplane flight: Aren't you afraid those terrible labor union racketeers will do something to your seven lovely children?

JFK: That's not me, that's my brother.

Seatmate: I hope your brother gets to be President.

JFK: That's not my brother, that's me.

Every morning Michael and I witnessed, knocking on doors around Los Angeles, spreading the word of Jehovah. As my brother's fame grew, he had to don convincing disguises, like a rubber fat suit he bought years later, around the time of *Thriller*. Adults were easily fooled by Michael incognito, but it was a rare child who didn't see through his costume in seconds.

LA TOYA JACKSON

For as jealous as I was of Freddy [my brother] at his birth, it wasn't long before I'd completely taken him under my wing. Not only was he a levelheaded and hard working little boy, he was an amiable costar in all our homespun productions.

LUCILLE BALL

I have an older brother, Larry, who has the same heart, the same kind of ability I do, and yet he's only 5-foot-8. This is a guy who will still play me one-on-one in a heartbeat. Despite all I've achieved in basketball, Larry believes he can win.

MICHAEL JORDAN, *For the Love of the Game: My Story*

I never tempted her with word too large,
But, as a brother to his sister, show'd
Bashful sincerity and comely love.

SHAKESPEARE, *Much Ado about Nothing. Act iv. Sc. 1.*

It was like therapy on stage every night for six months. A lot of
the same dynamics we were going through in life were going on
in that play [*True West*]. We got into some actual fights on stage,
and I enjoyed taunting him [Dennis]. I knew when I was really
mean to him on a particular night because he got to strangle me
at the end of the play. I could always tell how bad I was by how
seriously he strangled me.

RANDY QUAID

My brother Tove and I have always been big [*Star Wars*] fans. We used to play some of the early video games religiously, for an hour at a time, to make sure we became Jedi Knights.

HAYDEN CHRISTENSEN, Anaki Skywalker in *Star Wars*

My brother, Billy, reminds me of my father—in appearance, habits and attitudes. When we returned home from the Navy, Billy was only sixteen years old, and not at all inclined to take orders from an older brother. As soon as he finished high school, he left to join the Marine Corps ...Billy became a partner in our business, and now he runs it in my absence. Our friendship has grown steadily with the years, and I realize that his willingness to operate our farms and warehouse has made it possible for me to hold public office.

JIMMY CARTER

Earthworm: She won't be coming down here with the spray. She'll be coming down here with a shovel. It happened to my brother. Split him right down the middle. Now I have two half-brothers.

Roald Dahl, James and the Giant Peach

There's no way Warren [Beatty] and I wouldn't become stars. It was bred into us by parents who were in competition with each other. One was driven to believe in success. The other was afraid of it.

Shirley MacLaine

Neither make thy friend equal to a brother; but if thou shalt have made him so, be not the first to do him wrong.

Hesiod, Works and Days

…my dad told me to love the older kids as brothers and sisters not as half-brothers and—sisters. I tried to, but I never knew if their warmth was really or merely a show to placate my dad. It was all very cordial between us, and superficial. Taking our cue from our father, we never talked about real feelings, so I don't really know what they thought back then of me or my dad.

AISSA WAYNE, daughter of John Wayne

I'd like to see Providence become kind of like the baby brother of Boston.

JOSEPH R. PAOLINO JR., Mayor of Providence, RI

A great 20th century philosopher, Charles Schulz, once had Linus observe that "Big sisters are the crabgrass on the lawn of life." I guess the same could be said of big brothers.

DARIEN FAWKES, *The Invisible Man*

He's my own brother. I mean, I know he got the same daddy as me, and the same mama....my whole life I been watching him—watched him get exactly where he is right now. But that's the way I feel about him, too.

RAHAMAN CLAY, brother of
Muhammad Ali, *The Tao of Muhammad Ali*

52

My brother Fred was always very, very good. He never did anything wrong—he was too much to bear. I was always in trouble, a real pain in the ass. I suppose I wasn't much fun to be around.

LUCILLE BALL

Harry plays the older brother, forever showing us the way. He tells me what the subject of my next book should be. He tells Bill how to make furniture. He tells us where we should vacation and what IRAs to buy, and so on. And he is forever explaining politics to me. His heart is good and he can't help himself, so Bill and I nod yes to everything he says and never do any of it.

STEPHEN E. AMBROSE, *Comrades*

That all men should be brothers is the
dream of people who have no brothers.

CHARLES CHINCHOLLES

When you find yourself getting irritated with someone, try
to remember that all men are brothers…and just give
them a noogie or an Indian burn.

JOHN M. WAGNER, *Don't Worry,
Be Crabby!: Maxine's Guide to Life*

Q. Senator, was your brother a guest at the White House in the final two weeks of your husband's administration?

A. He was a frequent guest at the White House, you know. He's my brother. I love my brother. I'm just extremely disappointed in this terrible misjudgment he made.

HILLARY RODHAM CLINTON, *New York Times*

He's her own brother,
But Sister is pleased
When the tables are turned
And Brother gets teased.

STAN and JAN BERENSTAIN, *The Berenstain
Bears and Too Much Teasing*

Some people might think that my mother is my biggest problem. She doesn't like turtles and she's always telling me to scrub my hands…But my mother isn't my biggest problem. Neither is my father. He spends a lot of time watching commercials on TV. That's because he's in the advertising business….

My biggest problem is my brother, Farley Drexel Hatcher. He's two-and-a-half years old. Everybody calls him Fudge…Fudge is always in my way. He messes up everything he sees. And when he gets mad he throws himself flat on the floor and he screams. And he kicks. And he bangs his fists. The only time I really like is when he's sleeping.

JUDY BLUME, *Tales of a Fourth Grade Nothing*

Now, I know she loved me all right, but I couldn't understand how she could ever like my older brother, Richard. He had orange hair that was like wire; he was covered in freckles and looked like a weasel with glasses.

PATRICIA POLACCO, *My Rotten Redheaded Older Brother*

My father is a bastard
My ma's an S.O.B.
My grandpa's always plastered
My grandma pushes tea
My sister wears a moustache
My brother wears a dress
Goodness gracious, that's why I'm a mess.

STEPHEN SONDEIM, West Side Story

"The woman still doesn't trust me."

"Why should she?" said his brother. "Your whole life's been a lie beginning with the time you stuffed all your papers down the sewer so you wouldn't be late for a Little League game."

ERMA BOMBECK, Family: The Ties that Bind...and Gag!

Boys are found everywhere—on top of, underneath, inside of, climbing on, swimming from, running around or jumping to. Mothers love them, little girls hate them, older sisters and brothers tolerate them, adults ignore them and Heaven protects them.

ALAN BECK, "What is a Boy"

Q: With all the changes that have gone on in your life, what do you see as the biggest turning point?
A: The birth of my brother. I was 3. My mother's water broke at my birthday party, which we were having early. So, they all left and went to deliver my brother...

BEN AFFLECK

We hope that the world will not narrow into a neighborhood before it has broadened into a brotherhood.

LYNDON BAINES JOHNSON

We will do everything together,
Just me and my little brother…

We will have bunk beds,
And I will have the top
'cause I'm bigger.

There are so many things we can do,
Just me and my little brother.

But first he'll have to learn how to walk.

MERCER MAYER, *Just Me and My Little Brother*

The story of my boyhood and that of my brothers is important
only because it could happen in any American family. It did, and
will again.

EARL EISENHOWER

There was nothing worse in the '70's than being thought of as a goody-goody. I hated it. I would have rebelled, except I knew my brothers would kill me if I did anything wrong.

MARIE OSMOND

The five Ringling brothers were Wisconsin boys. They had the circus in their blood. They never forgot the first show they put on. Young Al broke about every plate his mother owned doing a juggling act. Johnny tried dancing a jig. There was a menagerie too: a few chickens, some rabbits, a billy-goat, and—a horse. The horse's name was Zachary. The boys had bought him from an old veteran of the Mexican War for $8.42.

from "The Greatest Show on Earth" in *It Happened Here:*
Stories of Wisconsin by Margaret G. Henderson,
Ethel Dewey Speerschneider, and Helen L. Ferslev

[My brother] covered fires, fights and funerals, and anything else not important enough for the other more experienced reporters....He met a movie star and he wrote me three pages of raves about her.

MARCELLINE HEMINGWAY SANFORD, *At the Hemingways*

As a freshman, I was assigned to Northside campus but [my brother] Moon decided to remain with his classmates at the Southside school. It was probably fortunate for me that he did. Although he and I were close, he was still my older—and bigger—brother, and we had our share of brotherly fistfights and rivalries.

RONALD REAGAN

My brother, I knew, would not welcome this news. He was thirteen years older than I and considered it a minor miracle to have reached the age of twenty-five. "I don't know how I survived her cooking," he said as he was telling me about the years when he and Mom were living alone, after she had divorced his father and was waiting to meet mine. "She's a menace to society."

RUTH REICHL, *Tender at the Bone: Growing Up at the Table*

I wish I could swing up into the sky, up into the clouds. I might be able to fly around the whole world and not hear my brothers, Oliver and Eugene, cry in the middle of the night anymore. My mother says they're always hungry. She cries in the middle of the night, too. She says she's worn out nursing and feeding and changing and four boys is too much for her.

FRANK MCCOURT, *Angela's Ashes*

"You must not tell anyone," my mother said, "what I am about to tell you. In China your father had a sister who killed herself. She jumped into the family well. We say that your father has all brothers because it is as if she had never been born."

MAXINE HONG KINGSTON, *The Woman Warrior: Memoirs of a Girlhood Among Ghosts*

Ninety percent of the success is if the hosts have good chemistry and you can't get better chemistry than with siblings.

MARIE OSMOND

I don't have a dog. But my brother comes and he's pretty annoying.... He [Ben] always stole all of my clothes and socks and that kind of left me with a sense of betrayal.

CASEY AFFLECK

We were young together, we grew up together in Whitewater, Wisconsin, we have known each other longer than we have known anyone else except our parents. I can tell you without having to look whether Harry will hit a fastball or a curve or a change-up, or whether Bill will make a hook or a set shot or a left-handed layup. And they can tell you what I can and can't do on a tennis court, a football field or a basketball floor. And what else? What magazines they will read or newspapers. What clothes will appeal. Most of all, in our younger days, what girls would appeal to them, and who their friends would be. Such knowledge just is.

STEPHEN E. AMBROSE, *Comrades*

63

Dear Friends,
It has come to our attention that there has been a lot of confusion as it relates to our desires to continue performing together as a group. To dispel any rumors, we love working together as brothers and plan on continuing to do so.

Love,
The Osmond Brothers

All men are brothers, but, thank God,
they aren't all brothers-in-law.
ANTHONY POWELL, *A Dance to the*
Music of Time: At Lady Molly's

We must learn to live together as brothers
or perish together as fools.
MARTIN LUTHER KING

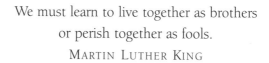